DAY PLANNER

M   T   W   Th   F   Sa   Su

To Do

Enthusiastic for

Appointments

Breakfast	Lunch	Dinner	Snack

Fitness	Mood

DAY PLANNER

Date: _____

M   T   W   Th   F   Sa   Su

To Do

_____

_____

_____

_____

_____

_____

_____

_____

_____

_____

_____

_____

_____

_____

Priorities

Enthusiastic for

Appointments

_____

_____

_____

_____

_____

Breakfast	Lunch	Dinner	Snack

Fitness

Mood

DAY PLANNER

Date: _____

M   T   W   Th   F   Sa   Su

To Do

Priorities

Enthusiastic for

Appointments

Breakfast

Lunch

Dinner

Snack

Fitness

Mood

DAY PLANNER

Date: _____

M   T   W   Th   F   Sa   Su

To Do

Priorities

Enthusiastic for

Appointments

Breakfast

Lunch

Dinner

Snack

Fitness

Mood

DAY PLANNER

Date: _____

M   T   W   Th   F   Sa   Su

To Do

_____

_____

_____

_____

_____

_____

_____

_____

_____

_____

Priorities

Enthusiastic for

Appointments

_____

_____

_____

_____

Breakfast

Lunch

Dinner

Snack

Fitness

Mood

DAY PLANNER

Date: _____

M   T   W   Th   F   Sa   Su

To Do

Priorities

Enthusiastic for

Appointments

Breakfast	Lunch	Dinner	Snack

Fitness	Mood

DAY PLANNER

Date: _____

M   T   W   Th   F   Sa   Su

To Do

_____

_____

_____

_____

_____

_____

_____

_____

_____

_____

_____

Priorities

Enthusiastic for

Appointments

_____

_____

_____

_____

Breakfast

Lunch

Dinner

Snack

Fitness

Mood

DAY PLANNER

Date: _____

M T W Th F Sa Su

To Do

_____

_____

_____

_____

_____

_____

_____

_____

_____

_____

_____

_____

Priorities

Enthusiastic for

Appointments

_____

_____

_____

_____

_____

Breakfast

Lunch

Dinner

Snack

Fitness

Mood

DAY PLANNER

Date: _____

M   T   W   Th   F   Sa   Su

To Do

Priorities

Enthusiastic for

Appointments

Breakfast

Lunch

Dinner

Snack

Fitness

Mood

DAY PLANNER

Date: _____

M   T   W   Th   F   Sa   Su

To Do

Priorities

Enthusiastic for

Appointments

Breakfast	Lunch	Dinner	Snack

Fitness	Mood

DAY PLANNER

Date: _____

M   T   W   Th   F   Sa   Su

To Do

Priorities

Enthusiastic for

Appointments

Breakfast	Lunch	Dinner	Snack

Fitness	Mood

DAY PLANNER

Date: _____

M T W Th F Sa Su

To Do

Priorities

Enthusiastic for

Appointments

Breakfast	Lunch	Dinner	Snack

Fitness	Mood

DAY PLANNER

Date: _____

M   T   W   Th   F   Sa   Su

To Do

_____

_____

_____

_____

_____

_____

_____

_____

_____

_____

_____

_____

_____

_____

Priorities

Enthusiastic for

Appointments

_____

_____

_____

_____

Breakfast	Lunch	Dinner	Snack

Fitness	Mood

DAY PLANNER

Date:

M T W Th F Sa Su

To Do

Priorities

Enthusiastic for

Appointments

Breakfast

Lunch

Dinner

Snack

Fitness

Mood

DAY PLANNER

Date: _____

M   T   W   Th   F   Sa   Su

To Do

_____
_____
_____
_____
_____
_____
_____
_____
_____
_____
_____
_____

Priorities

Enthusiastic for

Appointments

_____
_____
_____
_____

Breakfast

Lunch

Dinner

Snack

Fitness

Mood

DAY PLANNER

Date: _____

M T W Th F Sa Su

To Do

	Priorities

Enthusiastic for

Appointments

Breakfast	Lunch	Dinner	Snack

Fitness	Mood

DAY PLANNER

Date: _____

M T W Th F Sa Su

To Do

Priorities

Enthusiastic for

Appointments

Breakfast

Lunch

Dinner

Snack

Fitness

Mood

DAY PLANNER

Date: _____

M T W Th F Sa Su

To Do

Priorities

Enthusiastic for

Appointments

Breakfast

Lunch

Dinner

Snack

Fitness

Mood

DAY PLANNER

Date: _____

M   T   W   Th   F   Sa   Su

To Do

Priorities

Enthusiastic for

Appointments

Breakfast	Lunch	Dinner	Snack

Fitness	Mood

DAY PLANNER

Date: _____

M   T   W   Th   F   Sa   Su

To Do

Priorities

Enthusiastic for

Appointments

Breakfast

Lunch

Dinner

Snack

Fitness

Mood

DAY PLANNER

Date: _____

M T W Th F Sa Su

To Do

Priorities

Enthusiastic for

Appointments

Breakfast

Lunch

Dinner

Snack

Fitness

Mood

DAY PLANNER

Date: _____

M   T   W   Th   F   Sa   Su

To Do

Priorities

Enthusiastic for

Appointments

Breakfast

Lunch

Dinner

Snack

Fitness

Mood

DAY PLANNER

Date: _____

M   T   W   Th   F   Sa   Su

To Do

Priorities

Enthusiastic for

Appointments

Breakfast

Lunch

Dinner

Snack

Fitness

Mood

DAY PLANNER

Date: _____

M   T   W   Th   F   Sa   Su

To Do

Priorities

Enthusiastic for

Appointments

Breakfast

Lunch

Dinner

Snack

Fitness

Mood

DAY PLANNER

Date: _____

M   T   W   Th   F   Sa   Su

To Do

_____

_____

_____

_____

_____

_____

_____

_____

_____

_____

_____

_____

Priorities

Enthusiastic for

Appointments

_____

_____

_____

Breakfast

Lunch

Dinner

Snack

Fitness

Mood

DAY PLANNER

Date: _____

M T W Th F Sa Su

To Do

Priorities

Enthusiastic for

Appointments

Breakfast	Lunch	Dinner	Snack

Fitness	Mood

DAY PLANNER

Date: _____

M   T   W   Th   F   Sa   Su

To Do

Priorities

Enthusiastic for

Appointments

Breakfast	Lunch	Dinner	Snack

Fitness	Mood

DAY PLANNER

Date: _____

M T W Th F Sa Su

To Do

_____
_____
_____
_____
_____
_____
_____
_____
_____
_____
_____
_____
_____
_____

Priorities

Enthusiastic for

Appointments

_____
_____
_____
_____
_____

Breakfast

Lunch

Dinner

Snack

Fitness

Mood

DAY PLANNER

Date: _____

M   T   W   Th   F   Sa   Su

To Do

_____

_____

_____

_____

_____

_____

_____

_____

_____

Priorities

Enthusiastic for

Appointments

_____

_____

_____

_____

Breakfast

Lunch

Dinner

Snack

Fitness

Mood

DAY PLANNER

Date: _____

M T W Th F Sa Su

To Do

_____
_____
_____
_____
_____
_____
_____
_____
_____
_____
_____
_____
_____
_____

Priorities

Enthusiastic for

Appointments

_____
_____
_____
_____

Breakfast	Lunch	Dinner	Snack

Fitness	Mood

DAY PLANNER

Date: _____

M T W Th F Sa Su

To Do

Priorities

Enthusiastic for

Appointments

Breakfast

Lunch

Dinner

Snack

Fitness

Mood

DAY PLANNER

Date: _____

M   T   W   Th   F   Sa   Su

To Do

Priorities

Enthusiastic for

Appointments

Breakfast	Lunch	Dinner	Snack

Fitness	Mood

DAY PLANNER

Date: _____

M   T   W   Th   F   Sa   Su

To Do

_____

_____

_____

_____

_____

_____

_____

_____

_____

_____

_____

_____

_____

Priorities

Enthusiastic for

Appointments

_____

_____

_____

_____

Breakfast	Lunch	Dinner	Snack

Fitness

Mood

DAY PLANNER

Date: _____

M   T   W   Th   F   Sa   Su

To Do

	Priorities
	Enthusiastic for
	Appointments

Breakfast	Lunch	Dinner	Snack

Fitness	Mood

DAY PLANNER

Date: _____

M   T   W   Th   F   Sa   Su

To Do

_____
_____
_____
_____
_____
_____
_____
_____
_____
_____

Priorities

Enthusiastic for

Appointments

_____
_____
_____
_____
_____

Breakfast

Lunch

Dinner

Snack

Fitness

Mood

DAY PLANNER

Date: _____

M   T   W   Th   F   Sa   Su

To Do

Priorities

Enthusiastic for

Appointments

Breakfast

Lunch

Dinner

Snack

Fitness

Mood

DAY PLANNER

Date: _____

M   T   W   Th   F   Sa   Su

To Do

Priorities

Enthusiastic for

Appointments

Breakfast

Lunch

Dinner

Snack

Fitness

Mood

DAY PLANNER

Date: _____

M   T   W   Th   F   Sa   Su

To Do

Priorities

Enthusiastic for

Appointments

Breakfast

Lunch

Dinner

Snack

Fitness

Mood

DAY PLANNER

Date: _____

M   T   W   Th   F   Sa   Su

To Do

Priorities

Enthusiastic for

Appointments

Breakfast	Lunch	Dinner	Snack

Fitness	Mood

DAY PLANNER

Date: _____

M   T   W   Th   F   Sa   Su

To Do

Priorities

Enthusiastic for

Appointments

Breakfast

Lunch

Dinner

Snack

Fitness

Mood

DAY PLANNER

Date: _____

M   T   W   Th   F   Sa   Su

To Do

_____
_____
_____
_____
_____
_____
_____
_____
_____
_____
_____
_____
_____
_____

Priorities

Enthusiastic for

Appointments

_____
_____
_____
_____

Breakfast

Lunch

Dinner

Snack

Fitness

Mood

DAY PLANNER

Date: _____

M T W Th F Sa Su

To Do

Priorities

Enthusiastic for

Appointments

Breakfast	Lunch	Dinner	Snack

Fitness	Mood

DAY PLANNER

Date: _____

M   T   W   Th   F   Sa   Su

To Do

Priorities

Enthusiastic for

Appointments

Breakfast

Lunch

Dinner

Snack

Fitness

Mood

DAY PLANNER

Date: _____

M   T   W   Th   F   Sa   Su

To Do

Priorities

Enthusiastic for

Appointments

Breakfast

Lunch

Dinner

Snack

Fitness

Mood

DAY PLANNER

Date: _____

M   T   W   Th   F   Sa   Su

To Do

Priorities

Enthusiastic for

Appointments

Breakfast

Lunch

Dinner

Snack

Fitness

Mood

DAY PLANNER

Date: _____

M   T   W   Th   F   Sa   Su

To Do

Priorities

Enthusiastic for

Appointments

Breakfast

Lunch

Dinner

Snack

Fitness

Mood

DAY PLANNER

Date: _____

M   T   W   Th   F   Sa   Su

To Do

_____
_____
_____
_____
_____
_____
_____
_____
_____
_____
_____
_____
_____

Priorities

Enthusiastic for

Appointments

_____
_____
_____
_____

Breakfast

Lunch

Dinner

Snack

Fitness

Mood

DAY PLANNER

Date: _____

M   T   W   Th   F   Sa   Su

To Do

Priorities

Enthusiastic for

Appointments

Breakfast	Lunch	Dinner	Snack

Fitness	Mood

DAY PLANNER

Date: _____

M   T   W   Th   F   Sa   Su

To Do

_____
_____
_____
_____
_____
_____
_____
_____
_____
_____
_____
_____

Priorities

Enthusiastic for

Appointments

_____
_____
_____
_____

Breakfast

Lunch

Dinner

Snack

Fitness

Mood

DAY PLANNER

Date: _____

M T W Th F Sa Su

To Do

Priorities

Enthusiastic for

Appointments

Breakfast	Lunch	Dinner	Snack

Fitness	Mood

DAY PLANNER

Date: _____

M   T   W   Th   F   Sa   Su

To Do

Priorities

Enthusiastic for

Appointments

Breakfast

Lunch

Dinner

Snack

Fitness

Mood

DAY PLANNER

Date: _____

M T W Th F Sa Su

To Do

_____
_____
_____
_____
_____
_____
_____
_____
_____
_____
_____
_____
_____
_____

Priorities

Enthusiastic for

Appointments

_____
_____
_____
_____
_____

Breakfast	Lunch	Dinner	Snack

Fitness

Mood

DAY PLANNER

Date: _____

M T W Th F Sa Su

To Do

_____
_____
_____
_____

_____
_____
_____
_____
_____

_____
_____

Priorities

Enthusiastic for

Appointments

_____
_____

_____
_____
_____

Breakfast	Lunch	Dinner	Snack

Fitness

Mood

DAY PLANNER

Date: _____

M   T   W   Th   F   Sa   Su

To Do

Priorities

Enthusiastic for

Appointments

Breakfast

Lunch

Dinner

Snack

Fitness

Mood

DAY PLANNER

Date: _____

M   T   W   Th   F   Sa   Su

To Do

Priorities

Enthusiastic for

Appointments

Breakfast

Lunch

Dinner

Snack

Fitness

Mood

DAY PLANNER

Date: _____

M   T   W   Th   F   Sa   Su

To Do

Priorities

Enthusiastic for

Appointments

Breakfast	Lunch	Dinner	Snack

Fitness	Mood

DAY PLANNER

Date: _____

M   T   W   Th   F   Sa   Su

To Do

Priorities

Enthusiastic for

Appointments

Breakfast	Lunch	Dinner	Snack

Fitness	Mood

DAY PLANNER

Date: _____

M   T   W   Th   F   Sa   Su

To Do

Priorities

Enthusiastic for

Appointments

Breakfast

Lunch

Dinner

Snack

Fitness

Mood

DAY PLANNER

Date: _____

M   T   W   Th   F   Sa   Su

To Do

_____

_____

_____

_____

_____

_____

_____

_____

_____

_____

_____

_____

Priorities

Enthusiastic for

Appointments

_____

_____

_____

_____

Breakfast	Lunch	Dinner	Snack

Fitness	Mood

DAY PLANNER

Date: _____

M T W Th F Sa Su

To Do

Priorities

Enthusiastic for

Appointments

Breakfast

Lunch

Dinner

Snack

Fitness

Mood

DAY PLANNER

Date: _____

M T W Th F Sa Su

To Do

Priorities

Enthusiastic for

Appointments

Breakfast

Lunch

Dinner

Snack

Fitness

Mood

DAY PLANNER

Date: _____

M T W Th F Sa Su

To Do

Priorities

Enthusiastic for

Appointments

Breakfast	Lunch	Dinner	Snack

Fitness	Mood

DAY PLANNER

Date: _____

M   T   W   Th   F   Sa   Su

To Do

Priorities

Enthusiastic for

Appointments

Breakfast

Lunch

Dinner

Snack

Fitness

Mood

DAY PLANNER

Date: _____

M   T   W   Th   F   Sa   Su

To Do

_____
_____
_____
_____
_____
_____
_____
_____
_____
_____
_____
_____
_____
_____

Priorities

Enthusiastic for

Appointments

_____
_____
_____
_____
_____

Breakfast

Lunch

Dinner

Snack

Fitness

Mood

DAY PLANNER

Date: _____

M   T   W   Th   F   Sa   Su

To Do

Priorities

Enthusiastic for

Appointments

Breakfast

Lunch

Dinner

Snack

Fitness

Mood

DAY PLANNER

Date: _____

M   T   W   Th   F   Sa   Su

To Do

Priorities

Enthusiastic for

Appointments

| Breakfast | Lunch | Dinner | Snack |

Fitness

Mood

DAY PLANNER

Date: _____

M T W Th F Sa Su

To Do

_____
_____
_____
_____
_____
_____
_____
_____
_____
_____
_____
_____

Priorities

Enthusiastic for

Appointments

_____
_____
_____
_____

Breakfast

Lunch

Dinner

Snack

Fitness

Mood

DAY PLANNER

Date: _____

M T W Th F Sa Su

To Do

_____

_____

_____

_____

_____

_____

_____

_____

_____

_____

_____

_____

_____

Priorities

Enthusiastic for

Appointments

_____

_____

_____

_____

Breakfast

Lunch

Dinner

Snack

Fitness

Mood

DAY PLANNER

Date: _____

M T W Th F Sa Su

To Do

_____

_____

_____

_____

_____

_____

_____

_____

_____

_____

_____

_____

Priorities

Enthusiastic for

Appointments

_____

_____

_____

_____

Breakfast	Lunch	Dinner	Snack

Fitness	Mood

DAY PLANNER

Date: _____

M   T   W   Th   F   Sa   Su

To Do

Priorities

Enthusiastic for

Appointments

Breakfast

Lunch

Dinner

Snack

Fitness

Mood

DAY PLANNER

Date: _____

M   T   W   Th   F   Sa   Su

To Do

Priorities

Enthusiastic for

Appointments

Breakfast

Lunch

Dinner

Snack

Fitness

Mood

DAY PLANNER

Date: _____

M   T   W   Th   F   Sa   Su

To Do

Priorities

Enthusiastic for

Appointments

Breakfast	Lunch	Dinner	Snack

Fitness	Mood

DAY PLANNER

Date: _____

M T W Th F Sa Su

To Do

Priorities

Enthusiastic for

Appointments

Breakfast

Lunch

Dinner

Snack

Fitness

Mood

DAY PLANNER

Date: _____

M   T   W   Th   F   Sa   Su

To Do

Priorities

Enthusiastic for

Appointments

| Breakfast | Lunch | Dinner | Snack |

Fitness

Mood

DAY PLANNER

Date: _____

M T W Th F Sa Su

To Do

_____

_____

_____

_____

_____

_____

_____

_____

_____

Priorities

Enthusiastic for

Appointments

_____

_____

_____

_____

Breakfast	Lunch	Dinner	Snack

Fitness

Mood

DAY PLANNER

Date: _____

M   T   W   Th   F   Sa   Su

To Do

Priorities

Enthusiastic for

Appointments

Breakfast	Lunch	Dinner	Snack

Fitness	Mood

DAY PLANNER

Date: _____

M T W Th F Sa Su

To Do

Priorities

Enthusiastic for

Appointments

Breakfast

Lunch

Dinner

Snack

Fitness

Mood

DAY PLANNER

Date: _____

M T W Th F Sa Su

To Do

_____
_____
_____
_____
_____
_____
_____
_____
_____
_____
_____
_____
_____

Priorities

Enthusiastic for

Appointments

_____
_____
_____
_____

Breakfast

Lunch

Dinner

Snack

Fitness

Mood

DAY PLANNER

Date: _____

M   T   W   Th   F   Sa   Su

To Do

Priorities

Enthusiastic for

Appointments

Breakfast

Lunch

Dinner

Snack

Fitness

Mood

DAY PLANNER

Date: _____

M   T   W   Th   F   Sa   Su

To Do

Priorities

Enthusiastic for

Appointments

Breakfast	Lunch	Dinner	Snack

Fitness	Mood

DAY PLANNER

Date: _____

M   T   W   Th   F   Sa   Su

To Do

_____

_____

_____

_____

_____

_____

_____

_____

_____

_____

Priorities

Enthusiastic for

Appointments

_____

_____

_____

Breakfast	Lunch	Dinner	Snack

Fitness	Mood

DAY PLANNER

Date: _____

M   T   W   Th   F   Sa   Su

To Do

Priorities

Enthusiastic for

Appointments

Breakfast

Lunch

Dinner

Snack

Fitness

Mood

DAY PLANNER

Date: _____

M T W Th F Sa Su

To Do

Priorities

Enthusiastic for

Appointments

Breakfast	Lunch	Dinner	Snack

Fitness	Mood

DAY PLANNER

Date: _____

M   T   W   Th   F   Sa   Su

To Do

Priorities

Enthusiastic for

Appointments

Breakfast

Lunch

Dinner

Snack

Fitness

Mood

DAY PLANNER

Date: _____

M   T   W   Th   F   Sa   Su

To Do

_____

_____

_____

_____

_____

_____

_____

_____

_____

_____

_____

_____

_____

Priorities

Enthusiastic for

Appointments

_____

_____

_____

_____

Breakfast

Lunch

Dinner

Snack

Fitness

Mood

DAY PLANNER

Date: _____

M T W Th F Sa Su

To Do

Priorities

Enthusiastic for

Appointments

Breakfast

Lunch

Dinner

Snack

Fitness

Mood

DAY PLANNER

Date: _____

M T W Th F Sa Su

To Do

Priorities

Enthusiastic for

Appointments

Breakfast

Lunch

Dinner

Snack

Fitness

Mood

DAY PLANNER

Date: _____

M   T   W   Th   F   Sa   Su

To Do

Priorities

Enthusiastic for

Appointments

Breakfast

Lunch

Dinner

Snack

Fitness

Mood

DAY PLANNER

Date: _____

M T W Th F Sa Su

To Do

_____
_____
_____
_____
_____
_____
_____
_____
_____
_____
_____

Priorities

Enthusiastic for

Appointments

_____
_____
_____
_____

Breakfast

Lunch

Dinner

Snack

Fitness

Mood

DAY PLANNER

Date: _____

M T W Th F Sa Su

To Do

Priorities

Enthusiastic for

Appointments

Breakfast	Lunch	Dinner	Snack

Fitness	Mood

DAY PLANNER

Date: _____

M T W Th F Sa Su

To Do

Priorities

Enthusiastic for

Appointments

Breakfast

Lunch

Dinner

Snack

Fitness

Mood

DAY PLANNER

Date: _____

M   T   W   Th   F   Sa   Su

To Do

	Priorities

	Enthusiastic for

Appointments

Breakfast	Lunch	Dinner	Snack

Fitness	Mood

DAY PLANNER

Date: _____

M   T   W   Th   F   Sa   Su

To Do

Priorities

Enthusiastic for

Appointments

Breakfast

Lunch

Dinner

Snack

Fitness

Mood

DAY PLANNER

Date: _____

M   T   W   Th   F   Sa   Su

To Do

_____

_____

_____

_____

_____

_____

_____

_____

_____

_____

_____

_____

Priorities

Enthusiastic for

Appointments

_____

_____

_____

Breakfast	Lunch	Dinner	Snack

Fitness

Mood

DAY PLANNER

Date: _____

M   T   W   Th   F   Sa   Su

To Do

_____
_____
_____
_____
_____
_____
_____
_____
_____
_____
_____
_____

Priorities

Enthusiastic for

Appointments

_____
_____
_____
_____

Breakfast	Lunch	Dinner	Snack

Fitness	Mood

DAY PLANNER

Date: _____

M T W Th F Sa Su

To Do

Priorities

Enthusiastic for

Appointments

Breakfast

Lunch

Dinner

Snack

Fitness

Mood

DAY PLANNER

Date: _____

M   T   W   Th   F   Sa   Su

To Do

Priorities

Enthusiastic for

Appointments

Breakfast

Lunch

Dinner

Snack

Fitness

Mood

DAY PLANNER

Date: _____

M   T   W   Th   F   Sa   Su

To Do

Priorities

Enthusiastic for

Appointments

Breakfast

Lunch

Dinner

Snack

Fitness

Mood

DAY PLANNER

Date: _____

M T W Th F Sa Su

To Do

Priorities

Enthusiastic for

Appointments

Breakfast

Lunch

Dinner

Snack

Fitness

Mood

DAY PLANNER

Date: _____

M   T   W   Th   F   Sa   Su

To Do

_____
_____
_____
_____
_____
_____
_____
_____
_____
_____
_____
_____
_____

Priorities

Enthusiastic for

Appointments

_____
_____
_____
_____
_____

Breakfast

Lunch

Dinner

Snack

Fitness

Mood

Made in United States
North Haven, CT
02 January 2023

30499612R00062